DEFINITIONS AND TYPES OF INTERPERSONAL ATTRACTIONS IN RELATIONSHIPS.

BY

Dr TIMOTHY KESSINGTON

approval from the publisher or creator.

TABLE OF CONTENTS

ATTRACTION IN RELATIONSHIPS.

CONCLUSION.

ABOUT THE AUTHOR

Dr. TIMOTHY KESSINGTON is a licensed psychologist in the state of Texas. he is a certified counselor on marriage and relationship/mental health. He is passionate to the core to see people in relationships happy and couples achieve the best out of every relationship.

INTRODUCTION.

In relationships, interpersonal attraction is the intricate interaction of feelings and actions that bind people together. This introduction lays the groundwork for a deeper exploration of its definition, varieties, and complex components that add to the allure of intimacy and connection between individuals.

CHAPTER 1. WHAT IS INTERPERSONAL ATTRACTION? .

The notion of interpersonal attraction is an alluring power that creates emotional bonds between people. Physical beauty, common traits, intimacy, and reciprocal relationships are all important aspects of interpersonal attraction.

This intricate phenomenon underpins interpersonal relationships and is present in a wide range of social contexts, greatly influencing the dynamics that emerge and the degree of connection between people.

CHAPTER 2. INTERPERSONAL ATTRACTIVENESS AND ITS SIGNIFICANCE.

Human relationships are based on interpersonal attraction, the power that pulls people together. Its many manifestations, from similar interests to physical attractiveness, shape ties. It's critical to comprehend interpersonal attraction theory and what draws individuals to one another.

establishing preliminary contacts

The first spark that sparks ties between people is physical attraction. Facial symmetry, aesthetic attractiveness, and other physical attributes provide an instant attraction that encourages the investigation of more profound affinities.

 Even while this factor often loses importance over time, it nonetheless serves as a vital initiator in partnerships, laying the groundwork for further investigation.

<u>Creating Deep Connections.</u>

Social attraction is based on common interests, ideals, and personalities rather than just physical attraction. Common interests, passions, or ideals provide a strong basis for a deep and lasting relationship.

This mutual compatibility goes beyond surface-level factors and cultivates long-lasting relationships. The significance of social attraction is in its capacity to provide a foundation for relationships that transcend simple physical attraction, fostering strong and fulfilling ties.

<u>Reaching shared objectives</u>.
The core of attraction is
teamwork towards shared
objectives and initiatives, forging
a purpose. A special feeling of
connection and camaraderie is
fostered by the focus on
individual and group successes.

Certain types of attraction are
significant because they may help
create a common concept of
success and provide an alternative
viewpoint on the mechanics of
interpersonal interactions.

Activating the brain.

The significance of cerebral stimulation in relationships is emphasized by a few additional types of attraction. The depth of connection is increased by the shared desire to have talks, debates, and idea exchanges.

.

This kind of attraction highlights the value of mental compatibility and adds levels of complexity to relationships. One of the keys to a satisfying and long-lasting relationship is the capacity to intellectually challenge one another.

<u>strengthening of emotional ties</u>. Emotional attraction, the most important factor, creates the emotional foundation of partnerships. It is distinguished by a deep emotional bond that transcends surface-level encounters.

The capacity of emotional attraction to promote deep emotional resonance, empathy, and understanding among people is what makes it so significant. Being emotionally open and vulnerable fosters trust, which facilitates the development of close and profound relationships.

The comprehensive embroidery.

The majority of interpersonal attraction styles all add to the complex fabric of human relationships. Building and maintaining meaningful partnerships requires appreciating and respecting each component. Interpersonal attraction is significant because it offers a flexible base that takes into account many aspects of human connection.

Interpersonal attraction is essential to building long-lasting, rewarding relationships, whether via physical appeal, common interests, teamwork, intellectual stimulation, or emotional resonance.

CHAPTER 3.
INTERPERSONAL ATTRACTION TYPES AND THEIR DESCRIPTIONS.

Examine the many forms of interpersonal attraction to learn more about its nuances. This investigation explores the many elements that influence human interactions, ranging from the resonance of common interests to the magnetic pull of physical attraction. Learn about the subtle dynamics that promote closeness and create lasting connections.

A physical allure.

The first kind of attraction stemming from someone's appearance is physical attraction. This kind of attraction often incorporates a collection of attributes that influence one's perception of beauty.

What therefore draws individuals to one another? Aesthetic appeal is important; it includes aspects of interpersonal attraction such as proportionate features, clean skin, and symmetry on the face

.

Furthermore, chemistry and physical attraction are linked, producing a magnetic pull that makes people want to be physically near and in touch with one another.

Furthermore, cultural standards of beauty have a big impact on how people perceive physical appearance, which shapes their preferences and aspirations.

While physical attractiveness is important during the first stages of partnerships, as emotional attachments strengthen, their long-term relevance may decrease.

Social allure.
Social attraction is based on common interests, ideals, and

personalities rather than physical attractiveness. This kind of attraction is characterized by the following characteristics. First off, a common interest be it a passion, hobby, or set of values makes people feel a great deal more connected to one another.

Furthermore, social attraction is increased by personality and character trait complementarity, which lays the groundwork for long-lasting partnerships. A person's emotional connection to another person is reinforced by their shared knowledge and experiences.

Long-lasting relationships need social appeal because they offer a foundation that goes beyond physical desire.

Attraction of Task.

Task attraction is focused on working together on the same objectives or tasks, which adds a special touch to interpersonal relationships. Certain qualities are involved in this kind of attraction, which help define it. People who are attracted to one another by a similar task often discover ways to collaborate to achieve common goals.

A feeling of connection and camaraderie is fostered through cooperation and joint effort on tasks. Task attraction offers a distinct viewpoint on the dynamics of interpersonal relationships because of its emphasis on individual and collaborative successes.

<u>Intellectual appeal.</u>
The core elements of intellectual attraction are mental stimulation

and mutual respect for scholarly endeavours. A shared interest in conversing, debating, and sharing ideas is one of the traits linked to intellectual attraction.

People who are attracted to one another intellectually often find each other's ideas and points of view fascinating, which strengthens their bond. This kind of attraction emphasizes the value of intellectual stimulation and mental compatibility in the development of deep, lasting relationships.

Attraction on an emotional level
A transcendent force in human
interactions, emotional attraction
fosters a deep and personal tie
that adds colour to the brilliant
canvas of relationships. The
distinguishing characteristics of
this complex interaction include a
strong emotional resonance as
well as a depth of empathy and
mutual understanding that raises
relationships to a new level.

It goes below the surface,
negotiating weaknesses in
common to build a genuine, long-
lasting bond.

This kind of attraction shows up as an essential catalyst in the vast fabric of human interactions, entwining the strands of closeness and endurance and highlighting the priceless role that emotional ties play in the complex dance of interpersonal relationships.

CHAPTER 4. WHAT LEADS TO INTERPERSONAL ATTRACTION.

A multitude of factors impact the intricate phenomena known as the theory of interpersonal attraction.

These elements include the physical attractiveness of a person, the allure of similar interests or passions, the proximity that fosters connections, and the harmonic alignment of shared values that entwine people's lives.

Psychological theories that examine the many processes involved, such as the simple exposure effect and social exchange theory, provide light on the complex nature of attraction.

Beyond these assumptions, however, emotional reaction emerges as a critical factor that is closely linked to effective communication both of which are essential for developing strong bonds between people in the fascinating field of interpersonal attraction.

CHAPTER 5. FREQUENTLY ASKED QUESTIONS.

Recognize the subtleties of what binds individuals together, such as the significance of similar interests or the influence of physical attractiveness. Investigate the nuances of human connections and learn about the physics behind the magnetic pull that binds people together.

Which three kinds of interpersonal attraction are there?

There are three main forms of interpersonal attraction: task attraction, which stems from working together to achieve shared objectives; social attraction, which is based on similar interests and personalities; and physical attraction, which is based on looks.

Together, these dimensions influence relationship dynamics and represent the variety of factors that go into human connection.

Which four elements makes up an attraction?

Interpersonal attraction is influenced by four main factors: physical beauty, where appearance is important; proximity, which highlights similarities and highlights the influence of geographic closeness; and shared interests and values

Positive emotions are mutually exchanged in reciprocity.

These elements work together to add to the complexity of interpersonal interactions.

What kinds of attraction are there in interpersonal communication?

There are three different kinds of attraction in interpersonal communication: task attraction, which arises from working together towards shared objectives; social attraction, which is based on similar interests and personalities; and physical attraction, which is based on appearance.

Comprehending these elements facilitates the deciphering of the complex dynamics of interpersonal relationships and interactions within various social situations.

Which five elements make up interpersonal attraction?
According to social psychology, five main factors contribute to interpersonal attraction: physical

beauty, which is determined by
appearance proximity;
geographical proximity;
resemblance; and expressing
common interests and values.

good emotions shared by both
parties
competency, where respect for
abilities heightens the appeal
All of these components work
together to create a complex web
of interpersonal interactions.

CHAPTER 6. UNDERSTANDING ATTRACTION IN RELATIONSHIPS.

Examining interpersonal attraction showed that it has several facets, including physical attractiveness and common interests. To improve the dynamics of your relationships, think about getting professional help, such as counselling Additional helpful resources include courses on relationship development and effective communication. For satisfying and enduring relationships, invest in understanding and fostering these components.

CONCLUSION.

Effectively managing relationships requires an awareness of interpersonal attractions. The complexities within these interactions, from the wide spectrum of attractions physical, social, and task-related to the influence of individual and cultural variances, help us create deeper bonds. People may cultivate relationships that are healthier and more rewarding by understanding the relevance of attraction in many forms, which ultimately adds to the complexity and variety of human interactions.